BABY NAME:

THANK YOU

For Purchasing This "My First St. Patrick's Day High Contrast Baby Book"

Please Don't Forget To Leave Us An Honest <u>Review</u> And Share With Us Your Experience And How Can He Improve Even More.

THANK YOU FOR YOUR SUPPORT!

HELLO
BABY
ARE YOU
READY?

IT'S A BEAUTIFUL DAY

THE
GNOME SAYS
HAPPY
ST. PATRICK'S
DAY

CLOVER CUTIE.

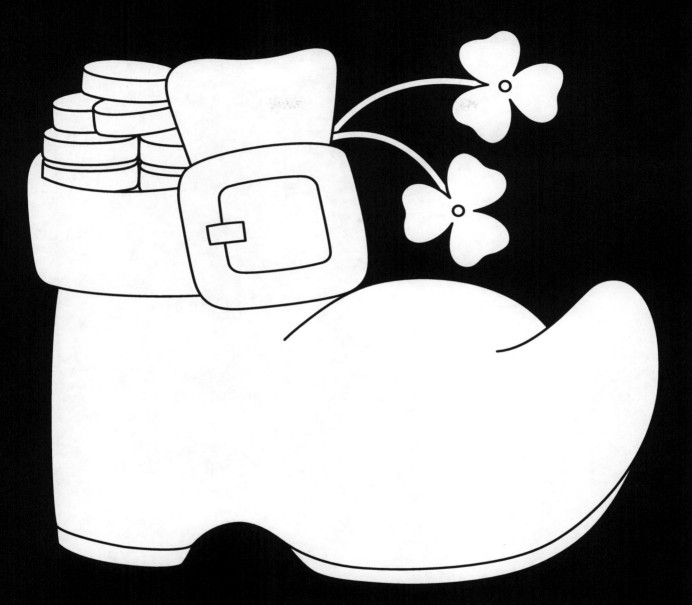

TINY FEET, BIG LUCK.

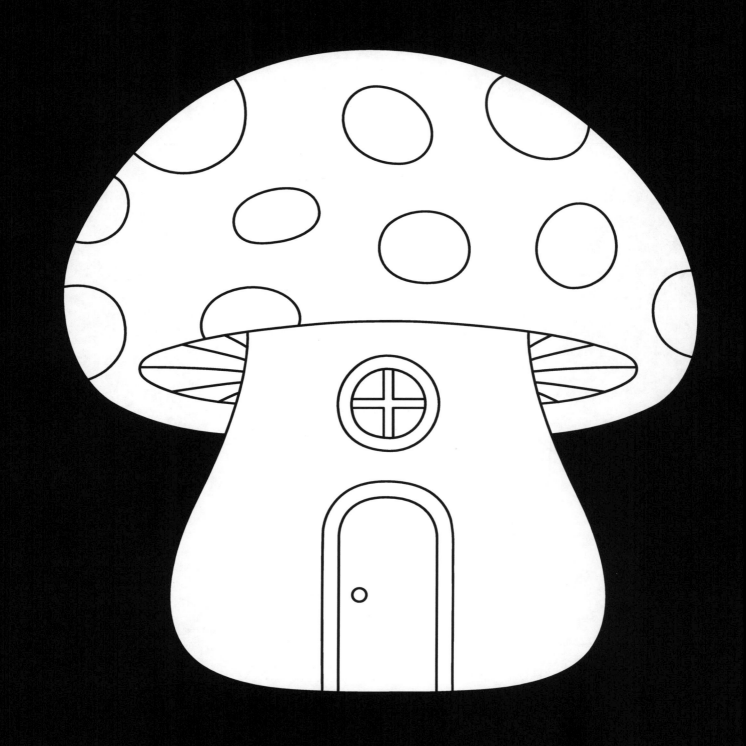

Made in the USA
Las Vegas, NV
12 January 2025

16273226R00020